Practice Test #1

Sentence Skills

Sentence Correction

Directions for questions 1–10
Select the best version of the underlined part of the sentence. The first choice is the same as the original sentence. If you think the original sentence is best, choose the first answer.

1. Children who aren't nurtured during infancy are more likely to develop attachment disorders, <u>which can cause persisting and severely problems</u> later in life.
   A. which can cause persisting and severely problems
   B. that can cause persisting and severe problem
   C. they can cause persistent and severe problem
   D. which can cause persistent and severe problems

2. While speed is a measure of how fast an object is moving, velocity measures how fast an object is moving <u>and also indicates in what direction</u> it is traveling.
   A. and also indicates in what direction
   B. and only indicates in which direction
   C. and also indicate in which directions
   D. and only indicated in what direction

3. Many companies are now using social networking sites like Facebook and MySpace <u>to market there service and product.</u>
   A. to market there service and product
   B. to market their services and products
   C. and market their service and products
   D. which market their services and products

4. An autoclave is a tool used mainly in hospitals <u>to sterilizing surgical tools and hypodermic needles</u>.
   A. to sterilizing surgical tools and hypodermic needles
   B. for sterilize surgical tools and hypodermic needles
   C. to sterilize surgical tools and hypodermic needles
   D. for sterilizing the surgical tool and hypodermic needle

5. <u>The bizarre creatures known by electric eels</u> are capable of emitting an incredible 600 volts of electricity.
   A. The bizarre creatures known by electric eels
   B. A bizarre creature known as electric eels
   C. The bizarre creatures known to electric eels
   D. The bizarre creatures known as electric eels

6. <u>A key factor taken into account during city planning is</u> where major services and amenities will be located.
   A. A key factor taken into account during city planning is
   B. Key factors taken into account during city planning is
   C. A key factor taking into account during city planning is
   D. Key factors, taken into accounting during city planning are

7. <u>Jupiter with its numerous moons, and Great Red Spot,</u> has been studied extensively by astronomers.
   A. Jupiter with its numerous moons, and Great Red Spot,
   B. Jupiter with, its numerous moons and Great Red Spot,
   C. Jupiter, with its numerous moons and Great Red Spot,
   D. Jupiter with, its numerous moons, and Great Red Spot,

8. Many gardeners are now making their own backyard compost, <u>which is not only cheap, but also helps to cut down on landfill waste.</u>
   A. which is not only cheap, but also helps to cut down on landfill waste
   B. which is not only cheaper, but also cuts down on landfill's waste
   C. which is, not only cheap, but also, helps to cut down on landfill waste
   D. which is not only done cheaply, but is also cutting down on landfills wastes

9. <u>The growth of the security industry can be large attributable</u> to the fact that people are less trusting of others than they once were.
   A. The growth of the security industry can be large attributable
   B. The growing of the securities industry can be largely attributable
   C. The growth on the security industry can be large attributed
   D. The growth of the security industry can be largely attributed

10. Claude Monet was a famous painter <u>who's well-known painting includes</u> Starry Night and Water Lilly Pond.
    A. who's well-known painting includes
    B. whose well-known painting including
    C. whose well-known paintings include
    D. who well-known paintings include

Construction Shift

Directions for questions 11–20

Rewrite the sentence in your head following the directions given below. Keep in mind that your new sentence should be well written and should have essentially the same meaning as the original sentence.

11. Bats and dolphins use a process known as echolocation, which means they emit and receive frequencies that can help them navigate through the dark night and murky waters, and also allows them to locate food sources like insects or fish.

Rewrite, beginning with

Locating food sources like insects or fish
The next words will be
   A. during which they emit and receive frequencies
   B. is done through a process known as echolocation
   C. helps them navigate through the dark night
   D. is done by bats and dolphins

12. Carbon dating is an accepted method used by archaeologists to figure out the age of artifacts, even though it may not be entirely accurate if samples are contaminated or if the objects to be dated are not extremely old.

Rewrite, beginning with

Even though carbon dating is not always entirely accurate,
The next words will be
   A. it is an accepted method
   B. objects to be dated
   C. to figure out the age
   D. samples are contaminated

13. Chemical changes are sometimes difficult to distinguish from physical changes, but some examples of physical changes, such as melting water, chopped wood, and ripped paper, are very easy to recognize.

Rewrite, beginning with

Melting water, chopped wood, and ripped paper
The next words will be
   A. are sometimes difficult to distinguish
   B. are very easy to recognize
   C. are chemical changes
   D. are some examples of physical changes

- 5 -

14. The theory of repressed memory was developed by Sigmund Freud, and it stated that all people store memories that cannot be accessed during daily life, but can be accessed through hypnotherapy and hypnosis.

Rewrite, beginning with

Developed by Sigmund Freud,
The next words will be
    A. it stated that all people
    B. that cannot be accessed
    C. hypnotherapy and hypnosis
    D. the theory of repressed memory

15. Romantic poetry is an important genre, and the works are easily distinguished from other types of poetry by several characteristics, including their focus on nature and the importance that is ascribed to everyday occurrences.

Rewrite, beginning with

A focus on nature and the importance that is ascribed to everyday occurrences
The next words will be
    A. are easily distinguished
    B. from other types of poetry
    C. are several characteristics
    D. is an important genre

16. The Sugar Act was implemented in 1764 by England, and it required individuals residing in the colonies of the United States to pay a tax on sugar, as well as on dyes and other goods.

Rewrite, beginning with

Implemented in 1764 by England
The next words will be
    A. the Sugar Act
    B. it required individuals
    C. in the colonies
    D. on sugar

17. Oil spill, as the phrase suggests, refers to the accidental introduction of oil into environments, and even though it can refer to land spills, the phrase is usually understood to refer to spills in water.

Rewrite, beginning with

<u>Even though the phrase "oil spill" is usually understood to refer to spills in water</u>
The next words will be
    A. as the name suggests
    B. it can refer to land spills
    C. and the introduction of oil
    D. known as oil spills

18. Radar was first used in 1904, and at that time all it was capable of was determining whether objects were present, but now it can determine the size and shape of an object, among other things, as well.

Rewrite, beginning with

<u>Although once only capable of determining the presence of objects,</u>
The next words will be
    A. radar was first used
    B. among other things
    C. radar can now determine
    D. the size and shape of an object

19. Placebos are often used in drug studies, and the effectiveness of a drug can be determined by measuring whether people with illnesses or diseases show significantly more improvement when they are given a real drug rather than a placebo.

Rewrite, beginning with

<u>By measuring whether people with illnesses show significantly more improvement when given a real drug,</u>
The next words will be
    A. the effectiveness of a drug
    B. placebos can be used in drug studies
    C. it is rather than a placebo
    D. is often used in drug studies

20. Employees value salary and good benefits in a job, but many also consider having an enjoyable job important, so it's difficult to say what the majority of people value most in a career.

Rewrite, beginning with

<u>While many people consider having an enjoyable job important,</u>
The next words will be
A.   it's what the majority of people
  B. it's difficult to say
  C. salary and good benefits
  D. other employees value

Reading Comprehension

Directions for questions 1–10
Read the statement or passage and then choose the best answer to the question. Answer the question based on what is stated or implied in the statement or passage.

1.   The Amazon Rainforest is one of the most important ecosystems in the world. However, it is slowly being destroyed. Areas of the rainforest are being cleared for farms and roads, and much of the wood is also being harvested and sold. There are several compelling reasons to protect this area. First, a significant number of pharmaceuticals are made from plants that have been discovered in the rainforest, and it's quite possible there are still important plants that have not yet been discovered. Secondly, the rainforest provides a significant portion of the world's oxygen and also absorbs great amounts of carbon dioxide. Without rainforests, global warming could accelerate.

The main purpose of the passage is
  A. to present the major reasons why the Amazon Rainforest is being destroyed.
  B. to explain why the Amazon Rainforest should be protected.
  C. to argue that rainforest destruction is a major cause of global warming.
  D. to discuss how the rainforest has helped in the development of medications.

2.   Howard Gardner was a psychologist best known for developing the theory of multiple intelligences. Basically, the theory states that the idea of general intelligence or overall intelligence is somewhat inaccurate. This is because people often show intelligence in different areas. He argued that there are actually different types of intelligence. One type of intelligence that Gardner identified was interpersonal intelligence. People who possess this type of intelligence relate and interact well with others. Intrapersonal intelligence, on the other hand, implies that people are in touch with their own feelings. They enjoy thinking about theories and developing their own thoughts and ideas. People who have linguistic intelligence learn best by taking notes and reading textbooks. These people usually excel in traditional academic environments, as many academic subjects stress these types of activities. The other types of intelligence are kinesthetic, musical, spatial, and logical/mathematical.

We can conclude from the passage that
   A. Gardner believed that linguistic intelligence was the most desirable type to have.
   B. most people who have a high level of intrapersonal intelligence do well in school.
   C. people who have a high level of interpersonal intelligence work well in groups.
   D. people who have mathematical intelligence would do the best on a standard IQ test.

3. The Internet has made life a whole lot easier for many people, but being online also brings with it very real risks. Hackers can steal personal and financial information. There are several precautions that computer users can take to minimize the level of risk that is involved with being online. One of the most obvious safety precautions is to purchase a good anti-virus and anti-spyware program. Passwords are also a very important part of online security, and several tips can help users create more secure passwords. First, they should be something that can easily be remembered, but they shouldn't be something others can guess easily. Your first or last name, phone number, or the name of your street are all bad choices, as people could learn this information quite easily. Longer passwords are more secure, and those that use a mixture of upper and lower case letters and a combination of letters and numbers are more secure than those that don't. Finally, passwords should be changed often. This can make remembering them more difficult, but the extra effort is worth the added security.

The main purpose of this passage is to
   A. discuss the major risks associated with Internet use.
   B. talk about the importance of anti-virus programs.
   C. outline important considerations for passwords.
   D. discuss why certain types of passwords shouldn't be used.

4. When people are conducting research, particularly historical research, they usually rely on primary and secondary sources. Primary sources are the more direct type of information. They are accounts of an event that are produced by individuals who were actually present. Some examples of primary sources include a person's diary entry about an event, an interview with an eyewitness, a newspaper article, or a transcribed conversation. Secondary sources are pieces of information that are constructed through the use of other, primary sources. Often, the person who creates the secondary source was not actually present at the event. Secondary sources could include books, research papers, and magazine articles.

From the passage it can be assumed that
   A. primary sources are easier to find than secondary sources.
   B. primary sources provide more accurate information than secondary sources.
   C. secondary sources give more accurate information than primary sources.
   D. secondary sources are always used when books or articles are being written.

5. Many people fail to realize just how crucial getting a good night's sleep actually is. It is usually suggested that adults get about seven hours of sleep every night, and younger children should get even more. Sleep has several benefits. First, it is believed to improve memory. This is one reason why it is always preferable to sleep the night before a test rather than stay up for the entire night to review the information. On a related note, sleep also improves concentration and mental alertness. Those who get sufficient sleep are able to concentrate on work tasks better and also react faster when they are driving a car, for example. Finally, people who get enough sleep have better immunity against illness. The reason for this is not fully understood, but researchers believe that an increase in the production of growth hormone and melatonin plays a role.

The main purpose of this passage is
   A. to talk about the benefits of sleep.
   B. to discuss how much sleep people should get.
   C. to identify which hormones can boost immunity.
   D. to present strategies for improving memory and concentration.

6. Feudalism was a type of social system that existed in parts of Europe during the Middle Ages. Essentially, there were several different classes within a feudal society. The king controlled all of the land in his jurisdiction. He divided this land among a few barons. The barons then divided up the land they were given and distributed it to knights. It was then split up again and distributed to serfs, who were the lowest members of feudal society. They were permitted to farm a small section of land, but they had to give a portion of their food to the knights in exchange for this privilege. They also had to give free labor to the knights who allowed them to use their land. Serfs had very few rights; they weren't even allowed to leave their land without permission from the knight who controlled the land. The system of feudalism ended when money began to be used as currency instead of land.

It can be concluded that
   A. serfs were in a better position when the economy changed to a money-based one.
   B. there were more knights in a typical feudal society than barons.
   C. the knights did not have to do anything for the barons in exchange for land.
   D. most feudal societies in Europe were ruled by more than one king.

7. A bird's feathers are extremely important, and when they clean and smooth them, it is known as preening. Birds in the wild preen their feathers on a regular basis. This is true of most captive birds as well, but not all. For example, some birds do not preen their feathers at all. This problem is most common in birds that are taken from their mothers at a very young age. Presumably, the absence of preening is due to the fact that they were never shown how to do it properly. A more common problem among captive birds is excessive preening. Some birds may pull out large numbers of their feathers or bite them down to the skin. It should be noted that wild birds never exhibit this kind of behavior. There are several suggestions about how the problem of excessive preening can be solved. Giving birds baths or placing them in an area that has more activity to prevent boredom are suggestions. However, these measures are often not sufficient to solve the problem.

The purpose of the passage is
    A. to give an overview of abnormal preening in birds.
    B. to compare captive birds to wild birds.
    C. to discuss why preening is important.
    D. to explain how excessive preening problems can be solved.

8. Hibernation in animals is an extremely fascinating phenomenon, one that biologists are not yet close to understanding fully. However, it is quite easy to understand why animals hibernate during the cold winter months. Usually, it is because their food is quite scarce during this time. Animals that are herbivores will find the winters extremely tough, because all of the vegetation will have died off by the time winter arrives. Hibernation is essentially a way of dealing with this food shortage. Animals like birds rely on seeds and small insects for sustenance. Obviously, these will also be quite scarce in the winter when the ground becomes covered and frozen. Many birds address their upcoming food shortage in quite a different way: they migrate to warmer areas where their sources of food will be plentiful.

The main reason animals hibernate is
    A. to travel to a warmer area where food will be more plentiful.
    B. to cut down on their food consumption during the winter months.
    C. to avoid the harsh weather that occurs during the winter months.
    D. to avoid food shortages that occur during the winter months.

9. At one time, the use of leeches to treat medical problems was quite common. If a person suffered from a snake bite or a bee sting, leeches were believed to be capable of removing the poison from the body if they were placed on top of the wound. They have also been used for blood letting and to stop hemorrhages, although neither of these leech treatments would be considered acceptable by present-day physicians. Today, leeches are still used on a limited basis. Most often, leeches are used to drain blood from clogged veins. This results in little pain for the patient and also ensures the patient's blood will not clot while it is being drained.

The main purpose of the passage is
   A. to discuss the benefits of using leeches to treat blocked veins.
   B. to give an overview of how leeches have been used throughout history.
   C. to compare which uses of leeches are effective and which are not.
   D. to explain how leeches can be used to remove poison from the body.

10. When online file-sharing programs emerged, the music industry changed forever. Perhaps the first widely-used music file sharing program was Napster. It allowed users to sign up to use the service at no charge. Then, they could download music files from other users all over the world by simply typing in what song or album they wanted. Obviously, this was bad news for music artists and record labels because they weren't making any profits from downloaded music. Eventually, Napster was shut down. While it later reinvented itself as a paying service, other free music-sharing sites cropped up almost immediately. Even though several sites and individual users have been charged, there are still countless individuals who log onto these sites to obtain free music.

The main problem associated with peer file-sharing sites is
   A. it is hard to locate users to criminally charge them.
   B. there are too many of them currently in existence.
   C. they prevent artists and labels from earning money.
   D. they allow users to sign up for the service free of charge.

Directions for questions 11–20
For the questions that follow, two underlined sentences are followed by a question or statement. Read the sentences, then choose the best answer to the question or the best completion of the statement.

11. Zoos are places that serve no other purpose than to allow greedy owners to make money.
    Some of the world's most endangered animals can be found in zoos, where they are protected from poachers and predators.

What does the second sentence do?
   A. It challenges the first.
   B. It provides an example.
   C. It supports the first.
   D. It restates the first.

- 12 -

12. Elephants are highly intelligent animals that are known to display several human-like behaviors.
When a member of their herd dies, elephants create graves for their fallen comrades, and have been known to visit burial sites years after the elephant's death.

What does the second sentence do?
   A. It provides a contrast.
   B. It provides an example.
   C. It restates the information from the first.
   D. It offers a solution.

13. Aerobic exercises, which include biking and running, offer several benefits, including better cardiovascular health.
Those who regularly walk or do other forms of aerobic exercise typically have a lower resting heart rate and suffer fewer heart problems.

What does the second sentence do?
   A. It offers a solution.
   B. It presents an example.
   C. It contradicts the information in the first.
   D. It expands on the information in the first.

14. Despite advancements in contraceptive technologies, teen pregnancy is still a huge problem in the United States.
Many schools are choosing not to teach students about contraception, and that means many may not be aware of how to obtain effective contraceptives.

What does the second sentence do?
   A. It expands on the information in the first.
   B. It offers a solution.
   C. It provides an explanation.
   D. It restates the information in the first.

15. Although it may seem impossible, solving a Rubik's Cube is quite doable if one knows about the various solving methods.
Manipulating the cube so that all of the corner pieces are in their correct positions and then essentially filling in the blanks is a time-consuming but effective solving methoD.

What does the second sentence do?
   A. It contrasts with the first.
   B. It offers an explanation.
   C. It restates the information in the first.
   D. It expands on the information in the first.

16. Many people now use digital devices such as PDAs to keep track of their schedules. PDAs are easy to use and, unlike day planners, there is no need to carry around a bulky notebook or search for a pen when you need to add something.

How are the sentences related?
   A. They provide a statement and an explanation.
   B. They present a problem and a possible solution.
   C. They present a principle and an example.
   D. They contradict each other.

17. DDT is a pesticide that is thought to adversely affect bird populations and contribute to the incidence of cancer in humans.
   In 1972, the use of DDT in the United States was banned.

What does the second sentence do?
   A. It supports the first.
   B. It states a result.
   C. It gives an example.
   D. It provides an explanation.

18. People who are concerned about the very real and sometimes serious side effects of conventional drugs are now turning to natural remedies.
   Natural remedies offer an alternative to drugs prescribed by doctors, which can often have serious adverse effects.

How are the two sentences related?
   A. They contradict each other.
   B. They support each other.
   C. They repeat the same information.
   D. They present a cause and an effect.

19. Students should study what they are passionate about when they attend university. Any individual considering university should research the job market and make decisions about what they will study based on current employment trends.

What does the second sentence do?
   A. It contradicts the first.
   B. It provides an example.
   C. It expands on the first.
   D. It offers a solution.

20. <u>Biological weapons, although considered by many to be relatively new, have actually been used by militaries for thousands of years.</u>
<u>In Greece, one military used biological warfare by throwing venomous snakes onto the ship of their enemy.</u>

What does the second sentence do?
   A. It offers a solution.
   B. It provides an example.
   C. It contradicts the first.
   D. It presents an effect.

Arithmetic Test

Solve the following problems and select your answer from the choices given. You may use the paper you have been given for scratch paper.

1. 9/81 is equivalent to which fraction?
    A. 1/18
    B. 1/9
    C. 3/9
    D. 5/9

2. 2 3/4 + 12 6/8 =
    A. 14 1/2
    B. 14 3/4
    C. 15 3/8
    D. 15 1/2

3. 789 – 32 =
    A. 737
    B. 747
    C. 757
    D. 767

4. 56 × 96 is closest to which value?
    A. 5,300
    B. 5,400
    C. 5,500
    D. 5,600

5. 456 / 23 =
    A. 19.83
    B. 19.93
    C. 20.03
    D. 20.63

6. 6/12 + 6/24 + 1/4 =
    A. 1/2
    B. 3/4
    C. 1
    D. 1 1/2

7. Which value is closest to 85% of 25?
    A. 16
    B. 18
    C. 20
    D. 22

8. 0.98 / 0.54 =
   A. 0.181
   B. 1.81
   C. 18.1
   D. 181

9. 1.45 × 0.99 =
   A. 1.44
   B. 2.44
   C. 3.44
   D. 4.44

10. 2.45 + 0.54 + 0.07 =
    A. 2.07
    B. 2.47
    C. 2.97
    D. 3.06

11. Which of the following represents the smallest value?
    A. 0.0009
    B. 0.00095
    C. 0.00089
    D. 0.000799

12. 5.36 - 0.78 =
    A. 4.38
    B. 4.58
    C. 5.37
    D. 5.48

13. Janet makes homemade dolls. Currently, she produces 23 dolls per month. If she increased her production by 18%, how many dolls would Janet produce each month?
    A. 27
    B. 32
    C. 38
    D. 40

14. Two cars are side by side. One is 3.9 meters long. The other is 6% shorter. How long is the second car?
    A. 3.5 meters
    B. 3.7 meters
    C. 3.9 meters
    D. 4.1 meters

15. A rectangle's width is 23 cm and its length is 9cm. What is its area?
    A. 32 cm²
    B. 104 cm²
    C. 207cm²
    D. 311 cm²

16. Three children decide to purchase a car for their parents. They will split the cost. One gives 1/4 of the cost; the other contributes 3/8 of the cost. What proportion of the cost will the third individual have to contribute towards the car?
    A. 1/4
    B. 3/8
    C. 1/2
    D. 5/8

17. Bruce is attending a conference that is 827 km from his home. If he travels at a speed of 64km/hour, approximately how long will it take him to reach his destination?
    A. 5 hours
    B. 9 hours
    C. 13 hours
    D. 17 hours

Elementary Algebra

Solve the following problems and select your answer from the choices given. You may use the paper you have been given for scratch paper.

1. $(-588 / 12) + (-36) =$
    A. -85
    B. -13
    C. 13
    D. 85

2. $865 + (-27) + (-85) + 26 =$
    A. 727
    B. 779
    C. 833
    D. 1003

3. If $| x - 15 | = 45$, what does x equal?
    A. -60 or 30
    B. -30 or 60
    C. -30
    D. -45

4. $5 \div (15 \div 3) - (7 \times 5) + 7 - 35 =$
   A. −70
   B. −62
   C. 62
   D. 70

5. Simplify the following.
   $(10x^3 + 2x^2 + 3) + (-5x^3 - 5x^2 + 3x - 9)$
   A. $15x^3 - 3x^2 + 3x - 6$
   B. $5x^3 - 7x^2 + 3x - 6$
   C. $5x^3 - 3x^2 + 3x + 6$
   D. $5x^3 - 3x^2 + 3x - 6$

6. Simplify the following.
   $$\frac{16x^3 - 32x^2 + 8x}{4x}$$
   A. $4x^3 - 8x^2 + 2x$
   B. $12x^2 - 28x^2 + 4$
   C. $4x^2 - 8x + 2$
   D. $4x^2 + 8x + 2$

7. Use factoring to simplify the following:
   $x^2 + 7x + 12$
   A. $(x + 6)(x + 2)$
   B. $(x + 4)(x + 3)$
   C. $(x + 6)(x + 1)$
   D. $(x + 5)(x + 2)$

8. If $y = 2$, what is the value of the following expression?
   $(y^9 / y^3) \times 2$
   A. 128
   B. 16
   C. 8192
   D. 1008

9. $7m + 43 = 160$
   What is the value of m?
   A. 110.0
   B. 16.7
   C. 29.8
   D. 819.2

10. A certain number of people purchased general concert tickets. They were $100 each. In addition, 25 people purchased front-row tickets, which were $200 each. If the total revenue from the concert was $34,000, how many people purchased general concert tickets?
   A. 150
   B. 338
   C. 390
   D. 290

11. Mary is evaluating her budget for the upcoming year. She has numerous employees, and they each make $700/week. In addition, she gives all employees a tax-free bonus of $100 each week. She figures out that in order to make a profit, what she pays out in salaries and bonuses each week cannot exceed her operating budget of $4,000. Which of the following inequalities represents a situation in which the company would make a profit?
   A. $800x \le 4000$
   B. $700x + 100 < 4000$
   C. $800x \ge 4000$
   D. $800x - 4000 \le 0$

12. $x^2 + x = 42$
   What is the value of x?
   A. $x = -7, -6$
   B. $x = 7, 6$
   C. $x = -7, 6$
   D. $x = 7, -6$

College Level Math Test

Solve the following problems and select your answer from the choices given. You may use the paper you have been given for scratch paper.

1. Simplify the following expression.
   $$\frac{25x^6y^7z^2}{5x^5y^2}$$
   A. $5x \cdot 5y^5 \cdot 5z^2$
   B. $5xy^5z^2$
   C. $20xy^5z^2$
   D. $5 xy^5z$

2. Expand the following expression.
   $(4x^3 - 6)(-3x^2 + 2x - 5)$
   A. $-12x^5 + 8x^4 - 20x^3 + 18x^2 - 12x + 30$
   B. $-12x^6 + 8x^3 - 20x^3 + 18x^2 - 12x + 30$
   C. $-12x^5 + 8x^4 - 20x^3 + 18x^2 - 4x - 11$
   D. $12x^5 + 8x^4 - 20x^3 + 18x^2 - 12x - 30$

3. Simplify the following expression.
$(16m^{16}y^4z^6/8m^8y^2z^3)^4$
   A. $8m^{12}y^6z^6$
   B. $2m^{12}y^2z^3$
   C. $8m^{32}y^8z^8$
   D. $16m^{32}y^8z^{12}$

4. $x^2 + 8x + 16 = 0$
   Solve for x.
   A. $x = -4, 4$
   B. $x = 4$
   C. $x = -4$
   D. $x = -2, 2$

5. Solve for x using the following system of equations.
   $3y + 10x = 23$
   $18y - 15x = 50$
   A. -1.17
   B. 1.17
   C. -3.75
   D. 3.75

6. Solve the following inequality.
   $8x + 7 \le -10x - 6$
   A. $x \ge -13/18$
   B. $x \le 6.5$
   C. $x \le -13/18$
   D. $x \ge 6.5$

7. Which of the following lines is parallel to the line $y = 3x - 12$?
   A. $3y - 9x = -36$
   B. $y = -1/3x - 12$
   C. $12y + 36x = 144$
   D. $y + 3x + 12 = 0$

8. In a coordinate plane, what is the distance between point A (4, 9) and B (15, 18)?
   A. 9
   B. $\sqrt{11}$
   C. 202
   D. $\sqrt{202}$

9. Calculate the point of intersection for the following lines.
$6x + 3y = 24$
$5y - 10 = 15x$
   A. (5.6, 1.2)
   B. (-1.2, 5.6)
   C. (1.2, 5.6)
   D. (-5.6, 1.2)

10. What is the y intercept of the line $7y + 14x - 42 = 0$?
   A. -6
   B. 6
   C. 2
   D. -2

11. What is the domain of the following function?
$f(x) = [(x + 10)/(x^2 - 9)]$
   A. All real numbers except -3 and +3
   B. All real numbers
   C. All real numbers greater than 3
   D. All real numbers less than -10

12. If $3^x = 24$, what is the value of x?
   A. 0.46
   B. 2.89
   C. 8
   D. 50.3

13. If $f(x) = 5x^3 + 8x^2 + 2x + 14$, what is the value of $f(3)$?
   A. 113
   B. 137
   C. 227
   D. 255

14. What is the domain of the function $f(x) = 2\cos x + 6$?
   A. All real numbers
   B. All values between -6 and 6
   C. All positive numbers
   D. All values between -2 and 2

15. What is the y intercept of the function $f(x) = 5*\cos(3x)$?
   A. (0, 3)
   B. (3, 0)
   C. (5, 3)
   D. (0, 5)

16. If $f(x) = 3\cos(x) + 5$, what is the value of $f(3°)$?
   A. 2
   B. 6
   C. 8
   D. 14

17. What is the determinant of the following matrix?
   $A = \begin{matrix} 8x & 7y \\ 3 & 2x \end{matrix}$
   A. $16x^2 - 21y$
   B. $10x + 10y$
   C. $16x^2 + 21y$
   D. $10x^2 - 10y$

18. What is the value of $7! - 3!$?
   A. 5,040
   B. 5,034
   C. 40
   D. 4

19. Evaluate $^{10}C_7$
   A. 20
   B. 70
   C. 105
   D. 120

20. A chef is given 7 different ingredients. His boss challenges him to come up with as many dishes as possible that use different combinations of four ingredients. What is the maximum number of permutations that are possible using the seven ingredients?
   A. 11
   B. 28
   C. 840
   D. 2401

Written Essay

Some people feel that video games actually promote intelligence. They say that strategy games force players to make strategic choices, plan ahead, and react in appropriate ways to challenges. Others feel that video games are simply a mindless pastime, and that time would be better spent doing something constructive like reading or participating in sports. Write an essay to a parent who is deciding whether they should allow their child to play video games. Take a position on whether video games are a valuable activity or simply a waste of time. Use arguments and examples to support your position.

Answer Explanations

Sentence Skills

Sentence Correction

1. D: Answer choice A is incorrect because *severely* is an adverb and not an adjective. B and C are incorrect because *problem* instead of the grammatically correct *problems* is used. D uses the correct, plural form *problems* and uses adjectives to describe the problems.

2. A: The sentence implies that *velocity* is used to indicate more than one value, which eliminates B and D. The phrase refers to velocity, which is singular, but the construction of choice C would correctly refer to a plural noun. Choice A agrees with the singular, noun and the *and* indicates that velocity is used to indicate more than one value.

3. B: Answer choice B uses the grammatically correct *their* instead of *there*. The *to* indicates the companies are using these sites for something, and *services* and *products* agree with each other because they are both plural.

4. C: Answer choice C states that an autoclave is a tool used *to sterilize*. A and B, which begin with *to sterilizing* and *for sterilize*, are not grammatically correct. D indicates that the machine is used to sterilize a single tool and needle, which does not make sense in the context of the sentence.

5. D: Answer choices A and C are incorrect because they imply that the bizarre creatures are something other than electric eels. The *a* in choice B does not agree with the plural *electric eels*. Choice D is best because it is grammatically correct and identifies electric eels as the bizarre creatures being discussed in the sentence.

6. A: Answer choice B is incorrect because the plural *key factors* and the singular *is* do not agree. The *taking* in choice C makes it incorrect. Choice D has a misplaced comma. Choice A makes sense and the singular *a key factor* and *is* agree with each other.

7. C: Choice C is the only choice that has correctly placed commas. The *numerous moons* and the *Great Red Spot* both refer to the planet Jupiter, which is maintained in answer choice C.

8. A: Answer choice B is incorrect because of the misplaced apostrophe. C has two unnecessary commas. Answer choice D is too wordy, and *landfills wastes* sounds quite awkward. Answer choice A is succinct, the comma is in the correct place, and it expresses the information is a clear way that is not awkward.

9. D: Answer choices A and C are incorrect because *large* is used in front of *attributable* and *attributed*. Both of these phrases are grammatically incorrect. B describes *the growing of*

the securities industry, which is quite awkward. D is the best choice because it refers to *the growth of the security industry* and uses the phrase *largely attributed*, which is grammatically correct.

10. C: The correct way to refer to a person, in this case Monet, is through the use of the pronoun *whose*, which eliminates A and D. Two paintings are identified, so the plural form must be used, eliminating choice B. Choice C uses *whose* and *paintings*, indicating there is more than one, making it the correct choice.

Construction Shift

11. B: The original sentence indicates that bats and dolphins are able to do many things, including locating food sources like insects or fish through a process known as echolocation. Answer choice B best expresses the fact that locating food is accomplished through echolocation. Answer choice C cannot logically follow the phrase. Answer choices A and D do not tell how bats and dolphins locate food.

12. A: The new sentence begins with the phrase "even though," indicating that a contrast is being constructed. "Even though carbon dating is not always entirely accurate, it is still an accepted method" provides this contrast, while the other choices do not.

13. D: Melting water, chopped wood, and ripped paper are identified in the original sentence as examples of physical changes that are easy to distinguish from chemical changes. Therefore, answer choices A and C are entirely incorrect. Answer choice B indicates that these objects are easy to recognize, but the sentence should convey that they are examples of physical changes that are easy to recognize, making this choice somewhat inaccurate. Choice D is best because it identifies the previously mentioned objects as examples of physical changes.

14. D: The only phrase that describes something developed by Sigmund Freud is D.
Answer choice A does not identify what the *it* is referring to, and B cannot logically follow the given phrase. Answer choice C describes ways to access repressed memories, but these were not developed by Freud.

15. C: A focus on nature and ascribing importance to everyday occurrences are identified in the original sentence as important characteristics of Romantic poetry. Answer choice C clearly identifies them as characteristics, and is the only choice that can logically follow the given phrase.

16. A: The Sugar Act is identified in the first sentence as something that was implemented in 1764 by England. Therefore, answer choice A is the best choice. Answer choice B does not indicate what was implemented. Answer choice C indicates where but not what was implemented, and D does not tell the reader what was implemented.

17. B: The phrase "even though" indicates a contrast. Answer choice A is more of an agreement than a contrast. Answer choice C is somewhat redundant, and D cannot logically

follow the given phrase. Answer choice B provides a contrast because the given phrase talks about spills in water, while choice B talks about spills on land. It is also a logical choice because "it" in choice B refers to "the phrase" that is mentioned in the given phrase.

18. C: C is the only choice that provides a distinction between then and now. The given phrase says that radar was *once* used to determine the presence of objects, and C indicates that radar can *now* determine other things as well.

19. A: The word "by" indicates a cause/effect relationship. By measuring whether people respond significantly more favorably when given a real drug, something is being accomplished. Answer choices C and D do not imply this relationship. Answer choice B does not make logical sense in the context of the sentence. Answer choice A states "the effectiveness of a drug," which is a good choice because it could logically be followed with a phrase like "can be determined."

20. D: The word "while" is used to establish a contrast, making D the obvious choice. The given phrase speaks about *some people*, while D identifies *other employees*, which creates an effective contrast.

Reading Comprehension

1. B: Answer choices A and C are mentioned only briefly. D is discussed, but it falls under the more general purpose of the passage, which is discussing why the Amazon Rainforest is a valuable area that should be protected.

2. C: Answer choice A is not a logical conclusion because there is no indication that Gardner ranked the intelligences in any way. Answer choice B cannot be concluded from the passage, as there is no mention of the value placed on intrapersonal intelligences in a traditional academic environment. IQ tests are not mentioned at all, so we can not conclude anything about them based on this passage. Answer choice C is the correct choice. Those with interpersonal intelligence interact well with others, so it is reasonable to assume they would perform well in a group setting.

3. C: Answer choices A and B are touched upon only very briefly. Answer choice D is discussed, but it is encompassed by the broader purpose of the passage, which is to outline the most important considerations related to passwords.

4. B: Answer choice B is the most logical conclusion. The passage states that, "Primary sources are the more direct type of information. They are accounts of an event that are produced by individuals who were actually present." Therefore, it is reasonable to assume that an account prepared by someone who was present would be more accurate than one prepared by somebody decades later who had to rely on the accounts of others.

5. A: Answer choices B and C are mentioned only briefly, and D is not really discussed in the passage. The passage focuses mainly on discussing some of the major benefits of sleep, so that is the main purpose of the passage.

6. B: Answer choice B is the logical conclusion. The passage states that "The king controlled all of the land in his jurisdiction. He divided this among a few barons. The barons then divided up the land they were given and distributed it to knights." If the barons divided up their lands, it would stand to reason that each baron would distribute his land to several knights. Therefore, there would have to be more knights than barons.

7. A: Answer choice B is not correct, because wild birds are not discussed at length. Answer choice C is not really discussed, and D is touched upon only briefly. The passage focuses on lack of preening and excessive preening, which are both examples of abnormal preening behavior. The main purpose of the passage is to discuss abnormal preening in birds.

8. D: The passage states that "Animals that are herbivores will find the winters extremely tough, because all of the vegetation will have died off by the time winter arrives. Hibernation is essentially a way of dealing with this food shortage." Therefore, D is the correct answer. Answer choice A is the purpose of migration, and answer choices B and C are not mentioned.

9. B: Answer choices A, C, and D are all mentioned in the passage, but they are part of the overall purpose, which is to give an overview of how leeches have been used throughout history.

10. C: The passage states that "Obviously, this was bad news for music artists and record labels because they weren't making any profits from downloaded music." Therefore, answer choice C is the correct choice. None of the other choices are identified as problems associated with file-sharing sites.

11. A: The first sentence states that the only purpose of zoos is to allow greedy people to profit. The second sentence challenges the first, however, pointing out that a key purpose of zoos is to protect endangered animals.

12. B: The first sentence states that elephants are capable of human-like behaviors. The second sentence states that elephants bury their dead and visit graves, which provides examples of human-like behaviors.

13. D: The first sentence mentions that cardiovascular health is a benefit of aerobic exercise. The second sentence mentions low resting heart rates and fewer cardiovascular problems, which are signs of good cardiovascular health. Therefore, the second sentence expands on the information in the first.

14. C: The first sentence identifies a problem: persisting high rates of teen pregnancy in spite of advancements in contraceptive technology. The second sentence offers a possible explanation: young people aren't being informed about how they can access contraceptives.

15. D: The first sentence mentions that various solutions for solving a Rubik's cube exist. The second sentence explains one in greater detail. Therefore, the second sentence expands on the information in the first.

16. A: The first sentence states that many people use digital devices to keep track of their schedules. The second describes several key advantages of PDAs that could possibly explain their popularity. Therefore, the sentences provide a statement and an explanation.

17. B: The first sentence states that DDT is a substance believed to be harmful to people and wildlife. The second sentence states that its use was banned in the United States. This ban is a direct result of the discovery of the harm that DDT can cause.

18. C: The two sentences express the same idea, and no new information is added in the second sentence. Therefore, the two sentences repeat the same information.

19. A: The first sentence states students should make decisions about what they will study in university based on their interests. The second states they should make decisions based on the job market. The second sentence directly contradicts the first.

20. B: The first sentence states that biological weapons have been used by militaries for many years. The second sentence tells about an army that threw poisonous snakes onto the ships of their enemies. The second sentence provides an example of biological weapons that were used long ago.

Arithmetic Test

1. B: When the numerator and denominator of a fraction are divided or multiplied by the same number, the product is an equivalent fraction. In this case, the numerator and denominator of 9/81 can be divided by nine, giving 1/9.

2. D: 2 3/4 + 12 6/8 =
First, ensure both fractions have a common denominator:
2 6/8 + 12 6/8 =
14 12/8
12/8 is greater than one, so express it as a whole number and a fraction: 1 4/8
Add this value to 14.
14 + 1 4/8
15 4/8
Reduce 4/8 by dividing the numerator and denominator by 4.
15 1/2

3. C: 789 – 32 = 757

4. B: 56 × 96 = 5376
This value is closest to 5400.

5. A: 456 ÷ 23 = 19.826
Rounding up, we get 19.83

6. C: 6/12 + 6/24 + 1/4 =
The common denominator is 24.
12/24 + 6/24 + 6/24 = 24/24
= 1

7. D: First, calculate 85% of 25.
25 x 0.85 = 21.25
This value is closest to 22 (D).

8. B: 0.98 / 0.54 = 1.81

9. A: 1.45 × .99 = 1.4355
Rounding up, we get 1.44

10. D: 2.45 + 0.54 + 0.07 = 3.06

11. D: Numbers that are farther to the right of the decimal point are smaller. Since all of the numbers have three zeros in front of them (that is, they are in the ten-thousandths place), look at the first number that is not a zero. The smallest number will represent the smallest value. Since the first number in D is 7, the lowest number, D represents the lowest value.

12. B: 5.36 - 0.78 = 4.58

13. A: First, calculate 18% of 23.
23 × 0.18 = 4.14
Then, add this value (the increase) to the original value of 23.
23 + 4.14 = 27.14
Rounding off, we get 27.

14. B: First, calculate 6% of 3.9.
3.9 × 0.06 = 0.234
Then, subtract this value (the decrease) from the original value of 3.9.
3.9 − 0.234 = 3.666 meters
Rounding off, we get 3.7 meters

15. C: The formula for the area of a rectangle is length × width.
Therefore, A = l × w
        A = 9cm × 23cm
        A = 207cm^2

16. B: There are two fractions: 1/4 and 3/8.
To answer the question, they have to be added. The common denominator is 8.
2/8 + 3/8 = 5/8
With the first two people, 5/8 of the cost of the car is covered.
Now, the remaining portion of the car's cost must be calculated.
Using the common denominator of 8, we know that 1 = 8/8

Therefore, to calculate the remaining portion of the cost of the car:
8/8 – 5/8 = 3/8

17. C: The distance that is being traveled and the speed are known. To find the time, simply set up these values in the following way.
827 ~~km~~ x $\frac{1 \text{ hour}}{64 \text{ km}}$ = x (the number of hours the trip will take)

827/64 = 12.92 hours
Rounding off, we get 13 hours.

Elementary Algebra

1. A: (– 588 / 12) + - 36 =
Perform the operations inside the brackets first:
-49 + -36 =
Then, do any adding or subtracting, working from left to right. Adding a negative integer is the same as subtracting the number.
-49 – 36 = -85

2. B: 865 + -27 + -85 + 26 =
Adding a negative integer is the same as subtracting the number.
865 – 27 – 85 + 26 =
753 + 26 = 779

3. B: | x - 15 | = 45
This is an absolute value, indicating x – 15 can equal 45 or -45.
Therefore, we simply have to solve for x in both instances.
x – 15 = 45
x = 45 + 15
x = 60

x – 15 = -45
x = -45 + 15
x = -30
x = (-30,60)

4. B: 5 ÷ (15 ÷ 3) – (7 × 5) + 7 – 35 =
Perform any operations inside the brackets first.
5 ÷ (5) – 35 + 7 – 35 =
Then, do any multiplication or division, working from left to right.
1 – 35 + 7 – 35 =
Finally, do any addition or subtraction, working from left to right.
-34 + 7 – 35 =
-69 + 7 = -62

5. D: $(10x^3 + 2x^2 + 3) + (-5x^3 - 5x^2 + 3x - 9)$
Remove the brackets, making sure to pay attention to whether the values are positive or negative.
$10x^3 + 2x^2 + 3 - 5x^3 - 5x^2 + 3x - 9 =$
Combine like terms.
$5x^3 - 3x^2 + 3x - 6$

6. C: $\dfrac{16x^3 - 32x^2 + 8x}{4x}$

To simplify, each term in the numerator can be divided by $4x$ to eliminate the denominator. The law of exponents that indicates that $x^n/x^m = x^{n-m}$ must be observed.
We are left with: $4x^2 - 8x + 2$

7. B: $x^2 + 7x + 12$
This expression can be simplified by using factoring.
The factors are $(x + 4)(x + 3)$.
To check the answer, multiply the first, outside, inside, and last terms (FOIL).
$x^2 + 3x + 4x + 12$
Combine like terms.
$x^2 + 7x + 12$

8. A: $(y^9 \div y^3) \times 2$
Since we know that $y = 2$, it is simply a matter of substituting this value into the equation.
$(2^9 \div 2^3) \times 2$
$(512 \div 8) \times 2$
$64 \times 2 = 128$

9. B: $7m + 43 = 160$
To solve for m, isolate the variable.
$7m = 160 - 43$
$7m = 117$
$m = 117 \div 7$
$m = 16.7$

10. D: The value we are trying to find is the number of people who purchased general concert tickets. Let that be x. Since we know they were 100 dollars each, the total value can be represented as $100x$.
Knowing that 25 people purchased front-row concert tickets, which were $200 each, we can calculate the total amount of money spent on front-row concert tickets.
$25 \times \$200 = \$5,000$
Since we also know the total revenue, we can then construct an equation.
$100x + 5,000 = 34,000$
Then, it is simply a matter of solving for x.

$100x = \$34,000 - \$5,000$
$100x = \$29,000$

$x = 290$
This is the number of people who purchased general admission tickets.

11. A: Mary gives her employees a salary of $700 and a bonus of $100. Let the total number of employees be x. The total amount she pays out can be represented by $800x$. To make a profit, this amount cannot exceed her operating budget, which is $4,000.
Therefore, $800x \leq 4000$ represents the situation that would allow the company to make a profit.

12. C: $x^2 + x = 42$
To solve for x, bring the 42 to the other side of the equation.
$x^2 + x - 42 = 0$
Then, factor the equation.
$(x + 7)(x - 6) = 0$
Then, solve for x.
$x + 7 = 0$
$x = -7$
$x - 6 = 0$
$x = 6$
$x = (-7, 6)$

College Level Math Test

1. B: $\dfrac{25x^6y^7z^2}{5x^5y^2}$

To simplify, divide the numerator by the denominator. The law of exponents that indicates that $x^n/x^m = x^{n-m}$ must be observeD.

We are left with: $5xy^5z^2$

2. A: $(4x^3 - 6)(-3x^2 + 2x - 5)$
To expand this, all terms in the second expression must be multiplied by each of the terms in the first expression. The law of exponents, which states that $x^n \cdot x^m = x^{n+m}$, must be observeD.
$-12x^5 + 8x^4 - 20x^3 + 18x^2 - 12x + 30$
There are no like terms, so the expression can not be simplified any further.

3. D: $(16m^{16}y^4z^6/8m^8y^2z^3)^4$
First, simplify the expression within the brackets. The law of exponents, which states that $x^n/x^m = x^{n-m}$, must be observed.
We are left with $(2m^8y^2z^3)^4$
Evaluate this expression. The law of exponents, which states that $(x^n)^m = x^{n \times m}$, must be observed.
We are left with $16m^{32}y^8z^{12}$

4. C: $x^2 + 8x + 16 = 0$
To solve for x, simplify this equation through factoring.
$(x + 4)(x + 4) = 0$
$x + 4 = 0$
$x = -4$

5. B: $3y + 10x = 23$
$\qquad\quad 18y - 15x = 50$
To find the value of a variable using a system of equations, one of the variables must be eliminateD.   To eliminate y from these equations, first multiply the top equation by -6.
$-6(3y + 10x = 23)$
$-18y - 60x = -138$

Then, add the two equations to eliminate y.

$\qquad -18y - 60x = -138$
$+ \quad\underline{18y - 15x = 50}$
$\qquad\qquad -75x = -88$

Solve for x.
$-75x = -88$
$x = -88/-75$
$x = 1.17$

6. C: $8x + 7 \le -10x - 6$
To make the equation easier to solve, isolate the variable.
$8x + 10x \le -6 - 7$
$18x \le -13$
$x \le -13/18$

7. A: Parallel lines have the same slope.
We are given $y = 3x - 12$, which has a slope of 3.
This equation form is known as slope-intercept form, and is generically expressed
$y = mx + b$, in which m is slope and b is the y-intercept,
Choice A is $3y - 9x = -36$
To calculate the slope, we need to solve for y
$3y = 9x - 36$
Divide both sides by 3.
$y = 3x - 12$
This is the same slope as the one in the given equation, so this line is the one that is parallel.

8. D: Since we know two points, we can create a third point that creates a right triangle.
Point C will have the same y coordinate as point A (9) and the same x coordinate as point B (15). Knowing this, we can then calculate the distance between points A and C and C and B.
The distance between A and C is the change in x.
$= 15 - 4$

- 34 -

= 11

The distance between C and B is the change in y.

= 18 – 9

= 9

We now have two sides of our right triangle. Figuring out the third side (C) will give us the distance between A and B.

To solve this problem, it is necessary to use the Pythagorean Theorem, which states that in a right triangle, $a^2 + b^2 = c^2$.

Therefore, $11^2 + 9^2 = c^2$

$121 + 81 = c^2$

$202 = c^2$

$\sqrt{202} = c$

9. C: $6x + 3y = 24$

$5y - 10 = 15x$

To find the point of intersection, solve one of the equations for either x or y.

For the first:

$5y - 10 = 15x$

$5y = 15x + 10$

$y = 3x + 2$

Then, substitute this expression for y in the first equation:

$6x + 3y = 24$

$6x + 3(3x + 2) = 24$

$6x + 9x + 6 = 24$

$15x = 18$

$x = 18/15$

$x = 1.2$

This is the value of x at the point of interception.

To find the value of y at the point of interception, use the calculated value of x to solve for y.

$6x + 3y = 24$

$6(1.2) + 3y = 24$

$7.2 + 3y = 24$

$3y = 16.8$

$y = 16.8/3$

$y = 5.6$

The point of interception is (1.2, 5.6)

10. B: $7y + 14x - 42 = 0$

To find the y-intercept, let x equal 0 and solve for y.

$7y + 14x - 42 = 0$

$7y + 0 - 42 = 0$

$7y = 42$

$y = 6$

11. A: $f(x) = [(x+10)/(x^2 - 9)]$
The domain is all of the values that x can have.
Numbers cannot be divided by 0, so looking at this function, we know that the denominator cannot be equal to 0.
$x^2 - 9 \neq 0$
$x^2 \neq 9$
$\sqrt{x^2} \neq \sqrt{9}$
$x \neq 3$ or -3

12. B: $3^x = 24$
To get the x out in front, take the logarithm of both sides.
$\ln 3^x = \ln 24$
$x \ln 3 = \ln 24$
$x = \ln 24/\ln 3$
$x = 2.89$

13. C: $f(x) = 5x^3 + 8x^2 + 2x + 14$
To find $f(3)$, it is simply a matter of substituting 3 for x
$f(3) = 5(3^3) + 8(3^2) + 2 \times 3 + 14$
$f(3) = 135 + 72 + 6 + 14$
$f(3) = 227$

14. A: $f(x) = 2\cos x + 6$
The domain can be any real number. This curve will continue along the x-axis in both directions indefinitely.

15. D: $f(x) = 5 \cos(3x)$
A cosine curve usually intercepts the y-axis at $(0,1)$. However, this cosine curve has a vertical stretch of 5, meaning the y-value of the point of interception must be multiplied by 5.
Therefore $(0, 1 \times 5)$
The y-intercept is $(0,5)$

16. C: $f(x) = 3\cos(x) + 5$
To find $f(3°)$, it is simply a matter of substituting 3° for x.
$f(3) = 3\cos(3°) + 5$
$f(3) = 3 \times 0.9986 + 5$
$f(3) = 8$

17. A: $A = \begin{matrix} 8x & 7y \\ 3 & 2x \end{matrix}$
To find the determinant, multiply the top left corner by the bottom right corner. Then subtract the product of the bottom left corner and the top right corner.

$(8x \cdot 2x) - (7y \cdot 3)$
$16x^2 - 21y$

18. B: 7! – 3! =
To evaluate:
$(1×2×3×4×5×6×7) – (1×2×3) =$
$5,040 – 6 = 5,034$

19. D: $^{10}C_7$
Subtract the number after the C from the number before the C (10 - 7 = 3). This is how many terms will be in your numerator and denominator. For the numerator, start with the highest number.
Therefore, 10×9×8 will be the numerator.
For the denominator, start with the lowest number.
Therefore, 1×2×3 will by the denominator.
So, $^{10}C_7 = \dfrac{10×9×8}{1×2×3}$

$^{10}C_7 = \dfrac{720}{6}$

$^{10}C_7 = 120$

20. C: We can express this as $^7P_4$
7 is the number we will begin with, and four is the number of values we will use to come up with the answer.
Therefore, the number of combinations is 7×6×5×4 = 840

Practice Test #2

Sentence Skills

Sentence Correction

Directions for questions 1–10
Select the best version of the underlined part of the sentence. The first choice is the same as the original sentence. If you think the original sentence is best, choose the first answer.

1. If he stops to consider the ramifications of this decision, <u>it is probable that he will rethink his original decision a while longer</u>.
    A. it is probable that he will rethink his original decision.
    B. he will rethink his original decision over again.
    C. he probably will rethink his original decision.
    D. he will most likely rethink his original decision for a bit.

2. When you get <u>older," she said "you will no doubt</u> understand what I mean."
    A. older," she said "you will no doubt
    B. older" she said "you will no doubt
    C. older," she said, "you will no doubt
    D. older," she said "you will not

3. <u>Dr. Anderson strolled past the nurses, examining a bottle of pills.</u>
    A. Dr. Anderson strolled past the nurses, examining a bottle of pills.
    B. Dr. Anderson strolled past the nurses examining a bottle of pills.
    C. Examining a bottle of pills Dr. Anderson strolled past the nurses.
    D. Examining a bottle of pills, Dr. Anderson strolled past the nurses.

4. Karl and Henry <u>raced to the reservoir, climbed the ladder, and then they dove into</u> the cool water.
    A. raced to the reservoir, climbed the ladder, and then they dove into
    B. first raced to the reservoir, climbed the ladder, and then they dove into
    C. raced to the reservoir, they climbed the ladder, and then they dove into
    D. raced to the reservoir, climbed the ladder, and dove into

5. Did either <u>Tracy or Vanessa realize that her decision would be</u> so momentous?
    A. Tracy or Vanessa realize that her decision would be
    B. Tracy or Vanessa realize that each of their decision was
    C. Tracy or Vanessa realize that her or her decision would be
    D. Tracy or Vanessa realize that their decision would be

6. Despite their lucky escape, <u>Jason and his brother could not hardly enjoy themselves</u>.
   A. Jason and his brother could not hardly enjoy themselves.
   B. Jason and his brother could not enjoy themselves.
   C. Jason and Jason's brother could not hardly enjoy themselves.
   D. Jason and his brother could not enjoy them.

7. Stew recipes call <u>for rosemary, parsley, thyme, and these sort of herbs.</u>
   A. for rosemary, parsley, thyme, and these sort of herbs.
   B. for: rosemary; parsley; thyme; and these sort of herbs.
   C. for rosemary, parsley, thyme, and these sorts of herbs.
   D. for rosemary, parsley, thyme, and this sorts of herbs.

8. Mr. King, <u>an individual of considerable influence, created a personal fortune and gave back</u> to the community.
   A. an individual of considerable influence, created a personal fortune and gave back
   B. an individual of considerable influence, he created a personal fortune and gave back
   C. an individual of considerable influence created a personal fortune and gave back
   D. an individual of considerable influence, created a personal fortune and gave it back

9. <u>She is the person whose opinion matters the most.</u>
   A. She is the person whose opinion matters the most.
   B. She is the person to whom opinion matters the most.
   C. She is the person who matters the most, in my opinion.
   D. She is the person for whom opinion matters the most.

10. Minerals are nutritionally significant elements <u>that assist to make your body</u> work properly.
    A. that assist to make your body
    B. that help your body
    C. that making your body
    D. that work to make your body

Construction Shift

Directions for questions 11–20
Rewrite the sentence in your head following the directions given below. Keep in mind that your new sentence should be well written and should have essentially the same meaning as the original sentence.

11. The Burmese python is a large species of snake that is native to parts of southern Asia, although the snake has recently begun infesting the Florida Everglades and causing environmental concerns by devouring endangered species.

Rewrite the sentence, beginning with the phrase, *The Burmese python has recently caused environmental concerns in the Florida Everglades*. The words that follow will be:
    A. because it is devouring endangered species in Florida

B. where it has made a home for itself away from its origins in southern Asia

C. by leaving its native home of southern Asia with an infestation of its natural prey

D. and is altering the delicate balance of species in that area

12. In the wild, the Burmese python typically grows to around twelve feet in length, but in captivity the snakes can often grow much longer than that, to upwards of fifteen or twenty feet in length.

Rewrite the sentence, beginning with the phrase, *Burmese pythons in captivity can grow to be as long as fifteen or twenty feet*. The words that follow will be:

A. as a result of the controlled environment that allows them to eat more

B. while it is typically shorter in the wild

C. but in the wild are shorter and may only be twelve feet long

D. which is much longer than a python in the wild grows to be

13. Florida biologists and environmentalists blame the exotic animals industry for the snake's introduction into the Everglades, because many snake owners are unable or unwilling to continue taking care of the creature once it grows too large and becomes too expensive.

Rewrite the sentence, beginning with the phrase, *The Burmese python can grow large and become too expensive for snake owners to maintain*. The words that follow will be:

A. and Florida biologists and environmentalists blame the exotic animals industry

B. so the python has been introduced into the Everglades

C. leaving the exotic animals industry at risk in the United States

D. resulting in abandoned snakes that have infested the Everglades

14. Lawmakers called for action against owning Burmese pythons after a pet python got out of its cage in a Florida home and killed a young child while she was sleeping, a situation that left responsible snake owners objecting and claiming that this was an isolated event.

Rewrite the sentence, beginning with the phrase, *Responsible Burmese python owners have claimed that the death of a young child in Florida after a python attack was an isolated event*. The words that follow will be:

A. but lawmakers have called for action against owning the pythons

B. because the python accidentally got out of its cage and attacked the child

C. that does not reflect accurately on conscientious snake owners

D. resulting in angry lawmakers who called for a prohibition of Burmese pythons

15. Biologists were initially concerned that the Burmese python could spread throughout much of the United States, due to its ability to adapt to its environment, but recent evidence suggests that the snake is content to remain within the Everglades.

Rewrite the sentence, beginning with the phrase, *Recent evidence suggests that the Burmese python is content to remain within the Everglades*. The words that follow will be:

A. due to its ability to adapt to its environment
B. and comes as a surprise to biologists who believed the snake would spread outside Florida
C. despite concerns that the snake could spread throughout much of the United States
D. because it is unable to adapt to cooler environments outside of south Florida

16. The most prolific predator in the Florida Everglades has always been the alligator, which preys on local birds and wildlife, while the introduction of the Burmese python adds another, and often insatiable, predator to compete with the alligator.

Rewrite the sentence, beginning with the phrase, *The introduction of the Burmese python to the Everglades adds another predator to compete with the alligator.* The words that follow will be:
A. which has always been the most prolific predator in the Everglades
B. thus leaving the local birds and wildlife in serious danger of becoming endangered
C. and the alligator was never as serious a predator as the python has become
D. which does not have the python's reputation for being insatiable

17. Not only does the Burmese python compete with the alligator for prey, but it also competes with the alligator as prey, because pythons have been known to engorge full-grown alligators, thus placing the python at the top of the food chain and leaving them with no native predators in the Everglades.

Rewrite the sentence, beginning with the phrase, *The Burmese python is now at the top of the food chain in the Everglades and has no native predator.* The words that follow will be:
A. so it competes with the alligator as prey
B. as evidence shows that pythons are capable of engorging full-grown alligators
C. although the python still competes with alligators for prey
D. leaving the Everglades with a serious imbalance of predators

18. Biologists and environmentalists recognize the considerable dangers of the python's expansion in the Everglades as it consumes endangered creatures native to that area, and in one instance researchers were shocked to discover that the tracking device for a tagged rodent led them to the python who had already consumed the unlucky creature.

Rewrite the sentence, beginning with the phrase, *Researchers in the Everglades were shocked to discover that the tracking device for a tagged rodent led them to the python who had already consumed the unlucky creature.* The words that follow will be:
A. thus showing how the python is destroying endangered species within the Everglades
B. causing concerns that the python expansion might be more dangerous than biologists and environmentalists originally believed
C. which was one of the few of its species that had managed to survive the python expansion in the Everglades

D. leaving biologists and environmentalists to recognize the considerable dangers of the python's expansion in the Everglades

19. In an attempt at controlling the python, Florida dispatched hunters to destroy as many pythons as possible, but after several months of searching the hunters were only able to make a dent in the python population of thousands by killing several dozen.

Rewrite the sentence, beginning with the phrase, *The python population of thousands was reduced only be several dozen.* The words that follow will be:
   A. even after many months of searching for and destroying the creatures
   B. because the hunters were only given a few months for the task and needed more time to destroy as many pythons as possible
   C. after the hunters sent to destroy as many pythons as possible failed to make a dent in the number
   D. resulting in concerns that more hunters were needed to locate and destroy as many pythons as possible

20. Although eradication is preferred when non-native species are introduced into the United States, researchers have found that is it virtually impossible, and controlling the species becomes the only real option in avoiding the destruction of native habitats and endangered species.

Rewrite the sentence, beginning with the phrase, *Controlling an invasive species is the only real option in avoiding the destruction of native habitats and endangered species.* The words that follow will be:
   A. because the total eradication of non-native species that are introduced into the United States is virtually impossible
   B. because the total eradication of non-native species that are introduced into the United States is generally frowned upon
   C. although researchers prefer the total eradication of non-native species and continue to make efforts to destroy the python in the Everglades
   D. in spite of the many attempts at totally eradicating the non-native species that are introduced into the United States

Reading Comprehension

Directions for questions 1–10
Read the statement or passage and then choose the best answer to the question. Answer the question based on what is stated or implied in the statement or passage.

1. The so-called anti-aging industry is worth a staggering amount of money in North America. Women are sold all sorts of creams and ointments, and are promised that these will make them look younger over time. Unfortunately, these claims are entirely false. Lotions cannot penetrate to the inner layers of the skin where wrinkles typically form. Therefore, no over-the-counter creams are effective at erasing lines and wrinkles.

According to the author, the anti-aging industry
   A. targets its products at men and women equally.
   B. sells products that are highly effective.
   C. is still a relatively small industry.
   D. sells goods that do not do what they promise.

2. There is a clear formula that many students are taught when it comes to writing essays. The first is to develop an introduction, which outlines what will be discussed in the work. It also includes the thesis statement. Next comes the supporting paragraphs. Each paragraph contains a topic sentence, supporting evidence, and finally a type of mini-conclusion that restates the point of the paragraph. Finally, the conclusion sums up the purpose of the paper and emphasizes that the thesis statement was proven.

After the topic sentence,
   A. a thesis statement is included.
   B. supporting evidence is presented.
   C. the conclusion is stated.
   D. the author outlines what will be discussed.

3. The importance of a comfortable work space cannot be overstated. Developing a comfortable work environment is relatively simple for employers. Ergonomic chairs, large computer screens, personal desk space, and some level of privacy are all essential. This involves some expense, but not a great deal. Not surprisingly, employees are happier in this type of environment, but it is the employers who really benefit. Reduced sick time, higher levels of employee satisfaction, higher productivity, and more creativity have all been observed.

The main idea expressed in this passage is
   A. a comfortable work space is not as important as people say.
   B. developing a comfortable work space is easy.
   C. establishing a comfortable work space is not expensive.
   D. employers benefit greatly when they provide comfortable work spaces.
4. Planning weddings is tough. One important part of the planning process is choosing bridesmaid dresses. Although there used to be a lot of rules when it came to picking out

- 43 -

a color, many of them are not observed any more. However, one that is still observed is that the bridesmaids should not wear the same color as the bride. The most popular colors for bridesmaid dresses in recent years have been white and black.

It can be concluded that
    A. picking dresses is the hardest part of planning a wedding.
    B. many brides are choosing to wear colors other than white.
    C. most bridesmaids are allowed to choose their own dress.
    D. bridesmaids were not traditionally allowed to wear black.

5. Those so-called green fuels may not be as environmentally friendly as once thought. For example, producing natural gas is a much more labor intensive process than producing an equal amount of conventional gasoline. Also, producing natural gas involves burning fossil fuels. Transporting natural gas also involves burning fossil fuels.

The weakness of green fuels is that
    A. they are not as abundant as conventional fuel.
    B. they require a lot more work to produce.
    C. burning them releases fossil fuels.
    D. they must be transported greater distances.

6. The media has done a lot to promote racism in North America. For example, it was found that the majority of crimes discussed on the nightly news featured African American suspects. However, when the total number of crimes committed in North American was examined, it was found that white people were also suspects 50% of the time.

If the above information were true, it could be concluded that
    A. there are more white criminals than African American criminals.
    B. most people believe that African Americans commit more crimes.
    C. many crimes committed by white people are not discussed on the news.
    D. the total number of crimes committed has decreased in the last several years.

7. Many people feel that the use of stem cells in research is unethical. However, they fail to realize that such research could lead to cures for some of the world's most troubling diseases. Diseases like Parkinson's and MS could possibly be cured through the use of stem cells, and those with spinal cord injuries could possibly walk again. Therefore, it is entirely ethical to engage in stem cell research aimed at easing the suffering of those who have life-altering conditions.

The main purpose of the passage is
    A. to discuss why people believe stem cell research is unethical.
    B. to discuss the possible benefits of stem cell research.
    C. to identify diseases that have been cured through stem cell research.
    D. to argue that not conducting stem cell research is unethical.

8. Many people do not know the difference between precision and accuracy. While accuracy means that something is correct, precision simply means that you are able to duplicate results and that they are consistent. For example, if there was a glass of liquid that was 100 degrees, an accurate measurement would be one that was close to this temperature. However, if you measured the temperature five times, and came up with a measurement of exactly 50 degrees each time, your measurement would be extremely precise, but not accurate.

The term accurate results refers to
A. results that are correct.
B. results that are consistent.
C. results that can be duplicated.
D. results that are measurable.

9. Literacy rates are lower today than they were fifteen years ago. Then, most people learned to read through the use of phonics. Today, whole language programs are favored by many educators.

If these statements are true, it can be concluded that
A. whole language is more effective at teaching people to read than phonics.
B. phonics is more effective at teaching people to read than whole language.
C. literacy rates will probably continue to decline over the next 15 years.
D. the definition of what it means to be literate is much stricter now.

10. George Washington was a remarkable man. He was born in 1732. Shortly before becoming the President of the United States in 1789, Washington was an important leader in the American Revolutionary War from 1775 to 1783. After retiring, he returned to Mount Vernon in 1797. A short time later, John Adams made him commander in chief of the United States Army again. This was done in anticipation that the country might go to war with France.

Almost immediately after serving as a leader in the American Revolutionary War
A. Washington returned to Mount Vernon.
B. Washington was made commander in chief of the U.S. Army.
C. Washington became the President of the United States.
D. Washington decided to go into retirement.

11. The history of the samurai in Japan is believed to date back to the late 7th century during a period of administrative reform that greatly reorganized Japan. In 663, Japan lost the Battle of Hakusukinoe against the Tang Dynasty of China.

What does the second sentence do?
A. It undermines the first.
B. It explains the first.
C. It restates the first.
D. It refutes the first.

12. The reform process did not initially create the warrior system that later became the samurai. The bureaucrats known as samurai were administrative officials whose name came from a word that meant "to serve."

What does the second sentence do?
    A. It examines the first.
    B. It reaffirms the first.
    C. It clarifies the first.
    D. It defines a term.

13. During attempts to conquer the island of Honshu, the 8th- and 9th-century Emperor Kammu relied on his serf army to accomplish the task. The emperor used clan members from his aristocracy to succeed in adding Honshu to Japan.

What does the second sentence do?
    A. It explains the first.
    B. It undermines the first.
    C. It offers essential evidence.
    D. It classifies the main idea.

14. The aristocratic clan members represented a powerful force in Emperor Kammu's army, due to their horseback skills and knowledge of weaponry, and he dismissed them following the victory at Honshu. Kammu slowly lost power in the 9th century.

What does the second sentence do?
    A. It presents a new theory.
    B. It transitions to a new idea.
    C. It adds crucial information.
    D. It implies a consequence.

15. The aristocratic clans began establishing their social and political power within Japanese culture. The clan members made powerful marriages, created treaties with other clans, and placed themselves under the code of the Bushido.

What does the second sentence do?
    A. It offers a comparison.
    B. It classifies a system.
    C. It elaborates on an idea.
    D. It refutes the main idea.

16. The Bushido represents an ethical system that shaped the clan leaders into a warrior class, or the samurai. The code of the Bushido encouraged personal honor, the

responsibility of the warrior to the lord, and loyalty to the lord even to the point of death.

What does the second sentence do?
    A. It develops the first.
    B. It establishes an effect.
    C. It contrasts with the first.
    D. It establishes the main idea.

17. The samurai grew in political and social authority during the late 12th century and the early 13th century. In 1185, the samurai were successful during their participation in the Battle of Dan-no-Ura.

What does the second sentence do?
    A. It examines the first.
    B. It questions the main idea.
    C. It offers comparative detail.
    D. It suggests a cause.

18. By the end of the 13th century, the samurai grew to be more powerful than the aristocrats they were intended to support. The samurai loyalty to the lord, as required by the Bushido code, became a purely nominal fidelity.

What does the second sentence do?
    A. It undermines the main idea.
    B. It restates the point of the first.
    C. It counters the presented theory.
    D. It examines a supporting thought.

19. Eventually, the samurai were so successful that their warrior services were no longer as necessary as they had been in the past. The samurai began to turn to more artistic pursuits, such as writing poetry and composing music.

What does the second sentence do?
    A. It provides comparative detail.
    B. It establishes an argument.
    C. It elaborates on the main idea.
    D. It offers essential information.

20. Despite a commitment to honorable death, many samurai still feared the prospect of dying by violent means. The principles of Zen Buddhism that were practiced among the samurai included personal discipline, meditation, and self-realization.

What does the second sentence do?
    A. It calls supporting information into question.
    B. It elaborates on a theory presented in the first.

C. It suggests a cause and effect relationship.
D. It compares and contrasts two systems of thought.

Arithmetic Test

Solve the following problems and select your answer from the choices given. You may use the paper you have been given for scratch paper.

1. Which number can be divided by 7 with no remainder?
   A. 42
   B. 48
   C. 51
   D. 67

2. Which of the following is equal to 12.5%?
   A. $\dfrac{1}{4}$
   B. $\dfrac{1}{8}$
   C. $\dfrac{1}{12}$
   D. $\dfrac{1}{16}$

3. Which of the following numerals is not a prime number?
   A. 3
   B. 6
   C. 17
   D. 41

4. The number 5 is multiplied by its reciprocal. What is the result?
   A. 0
   B. 1
   C. 1/5
   D. 5

5. Solve: $\dfrac{11}{8} + 7 + \dfrac{3}{4} + \dfrac{4}{3} = ?$
   A. $12\dfrac{5}{8}$
   B. $11\dfrac{5}{12}$
   C. $12\dfrac{5}{3}$
   D. $10\dfrac{11}{24}$

6. Lauren had $80 in her savings account. When she got her paycheck, she made a deposit that brought the total to $120. By what percentage did the total amount in her account increase as a result of this deposit?
   A. 50%
   B. 40%
   C. 35%
   D. 80%

7. Round 17.188 to the nearest hundredth.
   A. 17.1
   B. 17.2
   C. 17.18
   D. 17.19

8. What number is 3 more than 20% of 70?
   A. 14
   B. 17
   C. 18
   D. 21

9. What number added to 23 makes a number equal to one half of 94?
   A. 21
   B. 23
   C. 24
   D. 26

10. What is the difference between 45 and the average of 20, 35, 45, and 20?
    A. 0
    B. 15
    C. 17
    D. 20

11. A rectangle is twice as long as it is wide. If the width is 3 meters, what is the area in m²?
    A. 12 m2
    B. 6 m2
    C. 9 m2
    D. 18 m2

12. Which number is 300% of the difference between 23 and 27?
    A. 4
    B. 75
    C. 12
    D. 25

13. Which of the following sums is the greatest?
    A. 3 + 4 + 16

B. 6 + 4 + 5 + 7

C. 4 + 5 + 9

D. 10 + 4 + 8

14. If an odd number is added to an even number, the result must be
   A. odd
   B. even
   C. positive
   D. zero

15. Which of the following numbers is greatest?
   A. 1/3
   B. 0.25
   C. 0.099
   D. 2/7

16. Bob spends $17.90 on sodas and snacks for his study group. The expenses are to be split evenly between five people. How much is each person's share?
   A. $3.45
   B. $3.58
   C. $3.65
   D. $3.73

17. A clothing store offers a red tag sale during which items are offered at 5% off the marked price. Margaret selects a dress with a marked price of $120. How much will she have to pay for it?
   A. $115
   B. $110
   C. $96
   D. $114

Elementary Algebra

Solve the following problems and select your answer from the choices given. You may use the paper you have been given for scratch paper.

1. If $3x + 5 = 11$, then $x = ?$
   A. 6
   B. 3
   C. 2
   D. 1

2. If $a = -6$ and $b = 7$, then $4a(3b + 5) + 2b = ?$
   A. 638
   B. -485
   C. 850

D. -610

3. 7 + (6 - 4)5 + 8 = ?
   A. 25
   B. 53
   C. -15
   D. -10

4. Which of these is a solution to the inequality $4x - 12 < 4$?
   A. $x < 2$
   B. $x > 2$
   C. $x > 4$
   D. $x < 4$

5. Which algebraic expression best represents the following statement: the number of books Brian read over the summer (B) is 2 less than 3 times the number of books his brother Adam read over the summer (A)?
   A. $B = 3A - 2$
   B. $B = 3A + 2$
   C. $A = 3B - 2$
   D. $A = 3B + 2$

6. Which of the following is true?
   A. -(-(-4) is greater than -3
   B. -(-7) is greater than -17 minus 10
   C. -4 is greater than the absolute value of -4
   D. -10 is greater than -(-(-15)

7. Solve the equation: $2^3 + (4 + 1)$.
   A. 9
   B. 13
   C. 15
   D. 21

8. Juan got grades of 68 and 73 on his first two math tests. What grade must he get on the third test if all are weighted equally and he wants to raise his grade to a 75 average?
   A. 84
   B. 82
   C. 80
   D. 78

9. Vivian has $50. She goes to the store and buys a calculator. then she buys a book that costs half what the calculator cost. Then she buys a pen that costs half what the book cost. She has $15 left. How much did she spend on the calculator?
   A. $14
   B. $15

- 52 -

C. $18
D. $20

10. A leaky faucet drips at the rate of 2 drops per second. Each drop is 0.025 mL (milliliters). How many liters of water does the faucet leak per year (a year is 365 days)?
    A. 3,153.6
    B. 1,576.8
    C. 1,688.25
    D. 788.4

11. Richard sells cell phones. He is paid a commission of 10% for every phone he sells. The phones cost $140 each. How many phones must Richard sell in order to be paid $840?
    A. 40
    B. 50
    C. 60
    D. 70

12. What is the solution for the equation x/3 + 4 = 7
    A. 21
    B. 15
    C. 12
    D. 9

College Level Math Test

Solve the following problems and select your answer from the choices given. You may use the paper you have been given for scratch paper.

1. If $\dfrac{6^x}{6^2 + 6^2 + 6^2} = \dfrac{1}{3}$, then what is the value of x?
    A. 2
    B. 3
    C. 4
    D. 5

2. In a row of airplane seats, three people are seated next to each other. Felix and Marta are a couple and must sit next to each other. How many different seating arrangements are possible?
    A. 2
    B. 4
    C. 6
    D. 8

3. The radius of a circle with an area of 31 square units is doubleD.   What is the area of the new circle?
   A. 62 square units
   B. 93 square units
   C. 124 square units
   D. 132 square units

4. $3\sqrt{75} + 2\sqrt{3} = ?$
   A. $5\sqrt{25}$
   B. $17\sqrt{3}$
   C. $5\sqrt{225}$
   D. $5\sqrt{15}$

5. Examine (a), (b), and (c) and find the best answer. Consider only the magnitude of each measurement.
   (a) The perimeter of a rectangle with length of 6 cm and width of 4 cm
   (b) The perimeter of a square with sides 4 cm long
   (c) The area of a square with sides 4 cm long
   A. (b) > (c)
   B. = (b) = (c)
   C. (b) = (c)
   D. (b) < (c)

6. Simplify the following fraction: $[(x^2)^5 y^6 z^2] / [x^4(y^3)^4 z^2]$.
   A. $x^{40} y^{72} z^4$
   B. $x^6 y^{-6}$
   C. $x^3 y^{-1}$
   D. $x^{14} y^{18} z^4$

7. Tony has the following number of T-shirts in his closet:
   White - 5
   Black - 2
   Blue - 1
   Yellow – 3
   If Tony's electricity goes out, how many T-shirts would he have to pull out of his closet to make sure he has a yellow T-shirt?
   A. 4
   B. 8
   C. 9
   D. 11

8. If the two lines $2x + y = 0$ and $y = 3$ are plotted on a typical xy coordinate grid, at which point will they intersect?
   A. -1.5, 3
   B. 1.5, 3

C. -1.5, 0
D. 4,1

9. There are n musicians in a marching band. All play either a drum or a brass instrument. If p represents the fraction of musicians playing drums, how many play a brass instrument?
   A. $pn-1$
   B. $p(n-1)$
   C. $(p-1)n$
   D. $(1-p)n$

10. A package is dropped from an airplane. The height of the package at anytime t is described by the equation:
$$y(t) = -\frac{1}{2}at^2 + v_o + h_o$$

where y is the height, h_o is the original height, or the altitude from which it was dropped, a is the acceleration due to gravity, v_o is the original velocity and t is the time. The value of a is 32 ft/sec². If the airplane is flying at 30,000 feet, what is the altitude of the package 15 seconds after it is dropped?
   A. 29,520 ft
   B. 26,400 ft
   C. 22,800 ft
   D. 0 ft

11. A straight line with slope +4 is plotted on a standard Cartesian (xy) coordinate system so that it intersects the y-axis at a value of $y = 1$. Which of the following points will the line pass through?
   A. (2,9)
   B. (0,-1)
   C. (0,0)
   D. (4,1)

12. $|7-5|-|5-7|=?$
   A. 0
   B. 4
   C. 2
   D. -2

13. What is the surface area, in square inches, of a cube if the length of one side is 3 inches?
   A. 9
   B. 27
   C. 54
   D. 18

14. The following table shows the distance from a point to a moving car at various times.

d	Distance	50	70	110
t	Time	2	3	5

If the speed of the car is constant, which of the following equations describes the distance from the point to the car?
  A. $d = 25\,t$
  B. $d = 35\,t$
  C. $d = 55\,t$
  D. $d = 20\,t + 10$

15. Two angles of a triangle measure 15 and 70 degrees, respectively. What is the size of the third angle
  A. 90 degrees
  B. 80 degrees
  C. 75 degrees
  D. 95 degrees

16. A metal rod used in manufacturing must be as close a possible to 15 inches in length. The tolerance of the length, L, in inches, is specified by the inequality $|\,L - 15\,| \leq 0.01$. What is the minimum length permissible for the rod?
  A. 14.9 inches
  B. 14.99 inches
  C. 15.01 inches
  D. 15.1 inches

17. An MP3 player is set to play songs at random from the fifteen songs it contains in memory. Any song can be played at any time, even if it is repeated. There are 5 songs by Band A, 3 songs by Band B, 2 by Band C, and 5 by Band D. If the player has just played two songs in a row by Band D, what is the probability that the next song will also be by Band D?
  A. 1 in 5
  B. 1 in 3
  C. 1 in 9
  D. 1 in 27

18. An investigator working for a sporting league suspects that a ball used for one of the contests may have been filled with cork to alter the way it responds when hit. To test his suspicion, he weighs the ball. The density of cork is 3 gm/cm^3, whereas the normal filling has a density of 4 gm/cm^3. The diameter of the ball is 6 cm. If the ball has not been tampered with, how much should it weigh?
  A. 16.75 gm
  B. 113.9 gm
  C. 150.8 gm
  D. 211.45 gm

- 56 -

19. Which of the following expressions is equivalent to $(3x^{-2})^3$?
    A. $9x^{-6}$
    B. $9x^{-8}$
    C. $27x^{-8}$
    D. $27x^{-4}$

20. The town of Fram will build a water storage tank on a hill overlooking the town. The tank will be a right circular cylinder of radius R and height H. The plot of ground selected for the installation is large enough to accommodate a circular tank 60 feet in diameter. The planning commission wants the tank to hold 1,000,000 cubic feet of water, and they intend to use the full area available. Which of the following is the minimum acceptable height?
    A. 655 ft
    B. 455 ft
    C. 355 ft
    D. 255 ft

Written Essay

Prepare an essay of about 300-600 words on the topic below.

Merit pay for teachers is the practice of giving increased pay based upon the improvement in student performance. It is a controversial idea among educators and policy makers. Those who support this idea say that, with it, school districts are able to select and retain the best teachers and to improve student performance. Others argue that merit pay systems lead to teacher competition for the best students and to test-driven teaching practices that are detrimental to the overall quality of education.

In your essay, select either of these points of view, or suggest an alternative approach, and make a case for it. Use specific reasons and appropriate examples to support your position and to show how it is superior to the others.

Answer Explanations

Sentence Skills

Sentence Correction

1. C: The original sentence is redundant and wordy.

2. C: The syntax of the original sentence is fine, but a comma after *said* but before the open-quotation mark is required.

3. D: In the original sentence, the modifier is placed too far away from the word it modifies.

4. D: The verb structure should be consistent in a sentence with parallel structures.

5. A: The singular pronoun *her* is appropriate since the antecedents are joined by *or*. Also, the subjunctive verb form is required to indicate something indefinite.

6. B: The combination of *hardly* and *not* constitutes a double negative.

7. C: The plural demonstrative adjective *these* should be used with the plural noun *sorts*.

8. A: This sentence contains a number of parallel structures that must be treated consistently.

9. A: In this sentence, *whose* is the appropriate possessive pronoun to modify *opinion*.

10. B: Answer choice B is precise and clear. Answer choice A keeps the meaning, but is awkward and wordy. Answer choice C uses the wrong verb tense. Answer choice D would put the word *work* into the sentence twice. It is not completely incorrect, but it is not the best choice.

Construction Shift

11. A: Answer choice A best completes statement in the rewritten sentence by making the immediate connection between the environmental concerns and the reason for them. Answer choice B could work within the context of the sentence, but it does not create a sufficient link between the environmental concerns and their causes. Answer choice C provides information that is not contained within the original sentence, and answer choice D also adds information by noting that the "delicate balance" is altered. While this might be inferred from the original sentence, it cannot be added to the rewritten sentence.

12. C: Answer choice C accurately adds the statement of contrast about the python being shorter in the wild. Answer choice A adds information to the original sentence. Answer choice B is technically correct but does not contain as much information as answer choice C and is thus not the best choice. Answer choice D is also technically correct but does not provide the substance of the information that answer choice C contains.

13. D: Answer choice D creates the necessary link between the snake owners and the infestation of pythons in the Everglades. Answer choice A contains accurate information, but the sentence does not flow smoothly from one idea to the next. Answer choice B is true but is vague and fails to create a sufficient link between ideas. Answer choice C contains details that make no sense within the context of the sentence.

14. A: Answer choice A provides the sense of contrast that is contained within the original sentence by showing the differences between the responsible snake owners and the lawmakers. Answer choice B offers information that is contained within the original sentence but fails to provide a clear link between ideas. Answer choice C essentially repeats the information that is in the rewritten statement and is thus repetitive. Answer choice D, though correct, does not make a great deal of sense following up the information in the rewritten statement.

15. C: Answer choice C effectively restates the sentence by capturing the entire mood of the original. Answer choice A adds correct information, but it is incomplete with respect to the original idea. Answer choice B may be inferred to a degree, but there is not enough information in the original sentence to claim that the biologists were "surprised" about the results – only that they were "concerned" about the potential. Answer choice D adds information that is not within the original sentence.

16. A: Answer choice A correctly adds the necessary information about the alligator's traditional role within the Everglades. Answer choice B reassembles the information from the original sentence but does not provide the key detail about the alligator's place in the Everglades. Answer choices C and D add information that cannot be inferred from the original sentence.

17. B: Answer choice B provides the full information that is needed to complete the original idea. Answer choice A provides only partial information and is thus insufficient. Answer choice C is repetitive and does not offer any new information to complete the original idea. Answer choice D offers inferred information, but as this is not contained within the original sentence, it cannot be added.

18. D: Answer choice D adds the correct information about the concern that follows the python's expansion within the Everglades, without adding inferred information. Answer choice A is correct but is not necessarily effective in explaining the substance of the reason for concern. Answer choice B adds information that cannot be clearly inferred (i.e., what biologists and environmentalists originally believed about the python in the Everglades). Answer choice C adds information that has no place in the original sentence.

19. C: Answer choice C effectively links the ideas contained in the original sentence. Answer choice A is accurate but ineffective and incomplete, because it fails to explain *who* was doing the searching and destroying. Answer choices B and D add judgment statements that are not in the original sentence.

20. A: Answer choice A sufficiently links the ideas in the original sentence, connecting the reality of control with the hope for eradication. Answer choice B contradicts information that is not in the original sentence; that is to say, the original sentence states clearly that "eradication is preferred," not frowned upon. Answer choice C is partially correct but becomes incorrect with the added information about researchers continuing to search for means of eradication. Answer choice D contains correct information but does not encompass the full meaning of the original sentence and leaves out valuable information (i.e., the virtual impossibility of eradication).

Reading Comprehension

1. D: The passage states "Women are sold all sorts of creams and ointments, and are promised that these will make them look younger over time. Unfortunately, these claims are entirely false. Lotions can not penetrate to the inner layers of the skin, which is where wrinkles form." Therefore, these goods do not deliver what they promise.

2. B: The topic sentence is placed at the beginning of each supporting paragraph. Supporting evidence is presented after the topic sentence in each supporting paragraph. The passage states "Next come the supporting paragraphs. Each paragraph contains a topic sentence, supporting evidence, and finally a type of mini-conclusion that restates the point of the paragraph."

3. D: The main idea discussed in the passage is that employers benefit the most from establishing a comfortable work space. The author points out that it is not extremely expensive, then identifies all of the benefits for employers: better productivity, less absenteeism, etc.

4. B: It can be concluded that many brides are choosing to wear colors other than white based on two statements in the passage. First, we know that bridesmaids do not wear the same color as the bride. Secondly, it is stated that white is a popular color for bridesmaid dresses. Therefore, since the color of the bridesmaid dress is not the same as the bride's dress, it can be concluded that the bride's dress is not white.

5. B: Many green fuels require more work to produce than conventional fuels. The passage states "producing natural gas is a much more labor-intensive process than producing an equal amount of conventional gasoline. Producing natural gas also involves burning fossil fuels."

6. C: This conclusion can be made based on two statements. First, the passage states that "the majority of crimes discussed on the nightly news featured African American suspects." Second, "it was found that white people were also suspects 50% of the time." Therefore, if half of all suspects are white, but the majority of suspects on the news are African

- 60 -

American, it is reasonable to conclude that the news chooses not to report crimes that involve white suspects.

7. B: The main purpose of the passage is to discuss the possible benefits of stem cell research. The author states that many people feel it is unethical, but most of the passage is devoted to discussing the possible benefits of stem cell research. Cures for diseases and being able to repair spinal cord injuries are the possible benefits identified.

8. A: Accuracy is the same as correctness. The passage states "accuracy means that something is correct" and "if there was a glass of liquid that was 100 degrees, an accurate measurement would be one that was close to this temperature."

9. B: It can be concluded that phonics is a more effective way to learn to read for two reasons. First, the passage states that literacy rates are lower now than they were 15 years ago, meaning that more people knew how to read 15 years ago. Then, the passage states that phonics was the main way people learned how to read then. Therefore, based on these two facts, it can be concluded that phonics is more effective.

10. C: The passage states that "Shortly before becoming the President of the United States in 1789, Washington was an important leader in the American Revolutionary War from 1775 to 1783."

11. B: The second sentence explains the first by creating a link between the "period of administrative reform" and the failure at the Battle of Hakusukinoe. Answer choices A and D are incorrect, because the second sentence in no way undermines or refutes the first. Answer choice C is incorrect, because the second sentence does more than merely restate the first.

12. C: The second sentence clarifies the first by providing further detail about why the reform process in Japan "did not initially create the warrior system that later became the samurai." Answer choice A is incorrect, because it does not make sense in this context to say that the second sentence examines the first. Answer choice B is incorrect, because the second sentence does not just reaffirm the first: it provides further detail to explain the main point. Answer choice D is incorrect, because it limits the purpose of the second sentence. While the second sentence does indeed define a term, that is not its role. The second sentence clarifies the meaning of the first; in the process of doing so, it also happens to define a term.

13. B: The second sentence creates a conflict with the first, because the first sentence notes that the Emperor Kammu had a "serf army," while the second mentions his army of "clan members from his aristocracy." Without the historical explanation that Kammu dismissed the original army to create the aristocratic army, the second sentence appears to undermine the first. Answer choice A is incorrect, because instead of explaining the first sentence, the second sentence raises questions. Answer choice C is incorrect, because the second sentence could be said to require essential evidence but does not provide it. Answer choice D is incorrect, because it makes no sense in the context of the two sentences.

14. D: The second sentence implies a consequence: that the Emperor Kammu's power declined as a result of his choice to dismiss his aristocratic army. Answer choice A is incorrect, because the second sentence suggests a cause-and-effect relationship with the first, but this is not the same as presenting a new theory. (And without the context of what defines a new theory, answer choice A makes little sense.) Answer choice B is incorrect, because the second sentence seems to suggest a conclusion rather than the start of something new. Answer choice C is incorrect, because no context for crucial information is created between the two sentences.

15. C: The second sentence builds on the first by explaining how the aristocratic clans established themselves in Japanese culture by making marriages, creating treaties, and placing themselves under the Bushido. Answer choice A is incorrect, because it makes no sense in the context of the two sentences – no comparison is presented or made here. Answer choice B is incorrect, because no system is really classified; rather, the developing social position of the aristocratic clans is explained. Answer choice D is incorrect, because the second sentence supports and explains the main idea instead of refuting it.

16. A: As in question 5, the second sentence develops the primary idea of the first sentence by providing more detail about the Bushido and its meaning for the samurai. Answer choice B is incorrect, because it makes no sense; the possible effect is examined in the first sentence not the second if the Bushido were to be viewed as a type of cause. Answer choice C is incorrect, because no contrast is created within these sentences. Answer choice D is incorrect, because it describes the role of the first sentence instead of the second.

17. D: In the first sentence, a possible effect is created: the samurai became powerful during the late 12th century and the early 13th century. The second sentence follows with a mention of their success in a late 12th century battle. Therefore, the second sentence suggests a possible cause for the development of power. Answer choice A is incorrect, because it makes no sense in the context of the two sentences. Answer choice B is incorrect, because the second sentence does not attempt to question any part of the first. Answer choice C is incorrect, because no comparative information is offered in the second sentence.

18. B: The second sentence essentially restates the point of the first, that the samurai became more powerful than their lords and that the loyalty was largely in name-only by the end of the 13th century. Answer choice A is incorrect, because instead of undermining the main idea, the second sentence reaffirms it. In the same way, answer choice C is incorrect, because the second sentence does not counter, but rather confirm. Answer choice D is incorrect, because the role of the second sentence is to reiterate and not to examine.

19. C: The second sentence elaborates on the main idea by providing more information about what the samurai did since they were no longer needed as warriors. Answer choice A is incorrect, because the second sentence is not so much comparing as it is explaining. Answer choice B is incorrect, because the argument is established in the first sentence; the second sentence merely supports the argument. Answer choice D is incorrect, because it is difficult to determine within the limited context that is provided whether or not the

information in the second sentence is "essential." The main idea is presented in the first sentence and could stand on its own. The second sentence simply adds supporting detail.

20. C: The second sentence suggests a cause-and-effect relationship that cannot be obviously inferred from the first but that can still follow as a possible result. The first sentence notes that many samurai struggled with the idea of death, and the second sentence indicates that the samurai practiced Zen Buddhism – which offers the very teachings that warriors might use to handle the potential for violent death. Answer choice A is incorrect, because no supporting information is brought to bear. Answer choice B is incorrect, because the first sentence does not offer a theory; instead, it states a fact. Answer choice D is incorrect, because the two sentences have a cause-and-effect relationship but not a compare-and-contrast relationship.

Arithmetic Test

1. A: 7 x 6 = 42. Dividing any of the other choices by 7 leaves a remainder. For example, 7 goes into 51 (choice C) 7 times (7 x 7 = 49), with 2 left over.

2. B

Explanation: Percentage is equivalent to dividing by 100, so that $12.5\% = \dfrac{12.5}{100} = \dfrac{1}{8}$.

3. B: A prime number has only two whole integer divisors, 1 and itself. This is true of 3, 17, and 41. However 6 can be divided by 1, 2, 3, and 6. It is therefore not a prime number.

4. B: The reciprocal of 5 is $\dfrac{1}{5}$. When numbers are multiplied by their reciprocals, the result is always 1. Thus, $5 \times \dfrac{1}{5} = 1$.

5. D: To add mixed fractions, convert all the fractions so that they have the same denominator. This is done by finding the least common denominator, or LCD. In this case, since 8 equals 2 x 4, the LCD is 3 x 8 = 24. Now, convert all the fractions to a denominator of 24 by multiplying numerator and denominator by the same factors:
$$\frac{11(3)}{24} + \frac{7(24)}{24} + \frac{3(6)}{24} + \frac{4(8)}{24} = \frac{33 + 168 + 18 + 32}{24} = \frac{251}{24} = 10\frac{11}{24}$$

6. A: The percentage of increase equals the change in the account balance divided by the original amount, $80, and multiplied by 100. First, determine the change in the balance by subtracting the original amount from the new balance: $Change = \$120 - \$80 = \$40$. Now, determine the percentage of increase as described above: $Percent = \dfrac{\$40}{\$80} \times 100 = 50\%$.

7. D: To round to 1/100, leave two digits to the right of the decimal. To round digits greater than 5, round up to the next value of the preceding digit.

8. B: Twenty percent of 70 is $\dfrac{20}{100} \times 70 = 14$. Three more than 14 is 3 + 14 = 17.

9. C: One half of 94 equals 47. Since 47 – 23 = 24, C is the correct answer.

10. B: To compute the average, first total all the items in the list and then divide by the number of items in the list. This yields $\dfrac{20 + 35 + 45 + 20}{4} = \dfrac{120}{4} = 30$. The difference between 45 and 30 is 15.

11. D: The area of a rectangle is calculated as the product of the width and length. If the length is twice the width of 3 m, it must be 6 m long. Then, 3 x 6 = 18 m².

12. C: The difference 27 – 23 = 4, and 300% of 4 is 3 times 4, or 12.

13. A: The sum 3 + 4 + 16 = 23. The other choices are less. In particular, although it has more terms, choice B, 6 + 4 + 5 + 7 = 22, which is less than choice A.

14. A: An odd number can be considered as an even number N plus 1. Two even numbers added together produce an even number, so the result of adding an odd and an even number must be an even number plus 1, which is odd. For example, 4 + 3 = 7.

15. A: Convert all the numbers to fractions and compare. The number 0.099 can be rounded to 0.1. Then, the first 3 choices are: a) 1/3; b) 1/4; c) 1/100. Since the numerators are equal, the number with the smallest denominator is greatest, and that is 1/3. To compare that with choice D, note that 1/3 = 2/6 and 2/6 > 2/7.

16. B: Since five people are dividing $17.90, each person's share is calculated as $\dfrac{17.90}{5} = 3.58$.

17. D: The price is reduced by an amount equal to 5% of the original price, or $\dfrac{5 \times \$120}{100} = \$6$, so subtract $6 from the original price of $120 to calculate the sale price: $114.

Elementary Algebra

1. C: Since 11 – 5 = 6, then $3x = 6$, and $x = \dfrac{6}{3} = 2$.

2. D: First, compute the value enclosed by the parentheses, $3b + 5 = 3 \times 7 + 5 = 26$. Next, compute $4a = -24$. Note that a is negative, so that this product is negative as well. The product $4a(3b + 5)$ will therefore be negative as well, and equals -624. Finally, add the value of $2b$, or 2 x 7 = 14, to -624, to get the final answer $-624 + 14 = -610$.

- 64 -

3. A: Following the normal order of operations, the expression enclosed in the grouping symbols, or parentheses, must be evaluated first. This yields $7 + (2)5 + 8 = 7 + 10 + 8 = 25$.

4. D: Adding a constant to each side of the inequality does not change the sense of the inequality, so begin by adding 12: $4x < 4 + 12$, or $4x < 16$. Dividing each side of an inequality by a positive number does not change the sense of the inequality either, so now divide both sides by 4 in order to isolate the variable, x: $x < \dfrac{16}{4}$, or $x < 4$.

5. A: The correct answer is B = 3A - 2.

6. D: -10 is greater than -(-(-15)), which can also be written as -15.

7. B: $2^3 + (4 + 1) = 2 \times 2 \times 2 + 5 = 8 + 5 = 13$.

8. A: The average, or arithmetic mean, is computed by totaling all the measurements and dividing by the number of measurements. To obtain an average of 75 from 3 measurements, the measurements must total 3 x 75 = 225. Since 68 + 73 = 141, then 225 – 141 = 84 points are required on the third test.

9. D: If x is the cost of the pen, then, $2x$ is the cost of the book and $4x$ is the cost of the calculator. Vivian has spent x + 2x + 4x, or 7x. She started with $50 and had $15 left, so 50 – 7x = 15. Solving for x, $x = \dfrac{35}{7} = 5$, and the cost of the calculator was 4x = $20.

10. B: Since the rate is 2 drops per second and each drop is 0.025 mL, 0.05 mL of water is leaked per second. There are 60 x 60 x 24 x 365 seconds in one year. The amount of water lost in milliliters is $0.05 \times (60 \times 60 \times 24 \times 365) = 1{,}576{,}800$. Since there are 1,000 milliliters per liter, divide this number by 1,000. The result is answer choice B.

11. C: At 10%, Richard is paid $\$140 \times 10\% = \dfrac{10(140)}{100} = \$14$ for every phone he sells. To make $840, he must sell $\dfrac{840}{14} = 60$ phones.

12. D
Explanation: x/3 + 4 = 7, x/3 = 3, x = 9.

College Level Math Test

1. A: The denominator is equal to $3(6^2)$, so that the expression

becomes $\dfrac{6^x}{6^2+6^2+6^2} = \dfrac{6^x}{3(6^2)} = \dfrac{1}{3}$. If $6^x = 6^2$, these will cancel, leaving 1/3.

2. B: Fred and Marta may be seated on the left or the right, which yields two combinations. Within each of these arrangements, Fred may sit to the right of Marta or to her left. Therefore, the total number of seating arrangements is 2 x 2 = 4 possible combinations.

3. C: The area scales with the square of the radius, so if the radius increases in length by a factor of 2, the area will increase by 2^2, or 4. Since $Area = \pi r^2$, if the radius r is replaced with $2r$, this yields $Area = \pi(2r)^2 = 4\pi r^2$, which is 4 times the original area.

4. B: The first term is equivalent to $3\sqrt{3 \times 25} = 3(5\sqrt{3}) = 15\sqrt{3}$. Therefore the entire expression equals $15\sqrt{3} + 2\sqrt{3} = 17\sqrt{3}$.

5. C: The perimeter of a rectangle of length 6 and width 4 equals 2(6 + 4) = 20. The perimeter of a square of side 4 equals 4 + 4 + 4 + 4 = 16. And the area of a square of side 4 equals 4 x 4 = 16. Although the units for the measurement of area differ from those of the perimeters, the magnitude of the measurements for (b) and (c) are the same.

6. B: $(x^2)^5y^6z^2 / x^4(y^3)^4z^2 = x^{(2 \times 5)} - x^4 = x^{10} - x^4 = x^6$; $y^6 - y^{(3 \times 4)} = y^6 - y^{12} = y^{-6}$; $z^2 - z^2 = z^0$ or 0; so the answer is: $x^6 y^{-6}$.

7. C: He would have to pull out at least 9 (5 + 2 + 1 + 1) to make sure he has a yellow one.

8. A: Since the second line, $y = 3$, is a vertical, the intersection must occur at a point where $y = 3$. If $x = -1.5$, the equation describing the line is satisfied: $(2 \times [-1.5] + 3) = 0$

9. D: The fraction of those playing drums plus the fraction of those playing a brass instrument must total 1. So the number that play drums is pn, and the number playing brass must be $(1-p)n$.

10. B: Simply evaluating the expression yields

$$y(15) = -\frac{1}{2}(32)(15)^2 + 0 + 30{,}000 = -\frac{1}{2}(32)(225) + 0 + 30{,}000$$
$$= -3{,}600 + 30{,}000 = 26{,}400\text{ft}$$

11. A: As defined, the line will be described by the equation $y = 4x + 1$. Expression A fits this equation ($9 = 4 \times 2 + 1$). The others do not.

12. A: The vertical operators indicate absolute values, which are always positive. Thus, | 7-5 | = 2, and | 5-7 | = | -2 | = 2, and 2 – 2 = 0.

13. C: The surface of a cube is obtained by multiplying the area of each face by 6, since there are 6 faces. The area of each face is the square of the length of one edge. Therefore $A = 6 \times 3^2 = 6 \times 9 = 54$.

14. D: Inspection of the data shows that the distance traveled by the car during any 1-unit interval (velocity) is 20 units. However, the first data point shows that the car is 50 units from the point of origin at time 2, so it had a 10-unit head start before time measurement began.

15. D: The sum of angles in a triangle equals 180 degrees. Therefore solve for the remaining angle as 180 – (15 + 70) = 95 degrees.

16. B: The inequality specifies that the difference between L and 15 inches must be less or equal to 0.01. For choice B, | 14.99 – 15 | = | -0.01 | = 0.01, which is equal to the specified tolerance and therefore meets the condition.

17. B: The probability of playing a song by any band is proportional to the number of songs by that band over the total number of songs, or $\frac{5}{15} = \frac{1}{3}$ for Band D. The probability of playing any particular song is not affected by what has been played previously, since the choice is random.

18. C: The weight of the ball, W, is the product of the density, d, and the volume, V. Since a ball is a sphere, and the radius is half the diameter, the volume is $V = \frac{4}{3}\pi r^3$, so that

$$W = d \times \frac{4}{3}\pi r^3 = 4 \times \frac{4}{3}\pi \times 9 = 150.8 \text{ gm}.$$

19. C: Evaluate as follows:
$$(3x^{-2})^3 = 3^3 \times (x^{-2})^3 = 27 \times (\frac{1}{x^2})^3 = 27 \times \frac{1}{x^8} = 27x^{-8}$$

20. C: The volume of a right circular cylinder is equal to its height multiplied by the area of its base, A. Since the base is circular, $A = \pi R^2$, where R, the radius, is half the diameter, or 30 feet. Therefore,

$$V = H \times \pi R^2$$

Solving for H,

$$H = \frac{V}{\pi R^2} = \frac{1,000,000}{\pi \times 30^2} = \frac{1,000,000}{\pi \times 900} = 353.7 \text{ ft}$$

A and B are both greater than 355, so they do not represent the minimum acceptable height.

D is too low to hold the required volume.